counting in other languages

CW01583959

urdu

1	۱	aik [ay-k]	ایک
2	۲	tho [dho]	دو
3	۳	thin [teen]	تین
4	۴	char [chaa-r]	چار
5	۵	panch [paanch]	پانچ
6	۶	chae [chay]	چھ
7	۷	sath [saat-h]	سات
8	۸	ath [aat]	آٹھ
9	۹	nou [no-u]	نو
10	۱۰	dus [duss]	دس

swahili

1	moja [mo-jah]	
2	mbili [m-bee-lee]	
3	tatu [ta-too]	
4	nne [n-nay]	
5	tano [toh-no]	
6	sita [see-tah]	
7	saba [sah-bah]	
8	nane [nah-nay]	
9	tisa [tee-sah]	
10	kumi [koo-mee]	

hindi

1	१	aek [eck]	एक
2	२	do [doe]	दो
3	३	teen	तीन
4	४	chaar [chaar]	चार
5	५	panch [pa-nch]	पाँच
6	६	chhe [chay]	छे
7	७	saat	सात
8	८	aath [aat-h]	आठ
9	९	noun [no-u(ng)]	नौ
10	१०	das [duss]	दस

punjabi

1	੧	ick	ਇਕ
2	੨	dho	ਦੋ
3	੩	tin	ਤਿੰਨ
4	੪	chaa-r	ਚਾਰ
5	੫	panj	ਪੰਜ
6	੬	ch-hay	ਛੇ
7	੭	sut	ਸੱਤ
8	੮	ut-h	ਅੱਠ
9	੯	no(ng)	ਨੌਂ
10	੧੦	duss	ਦਸ

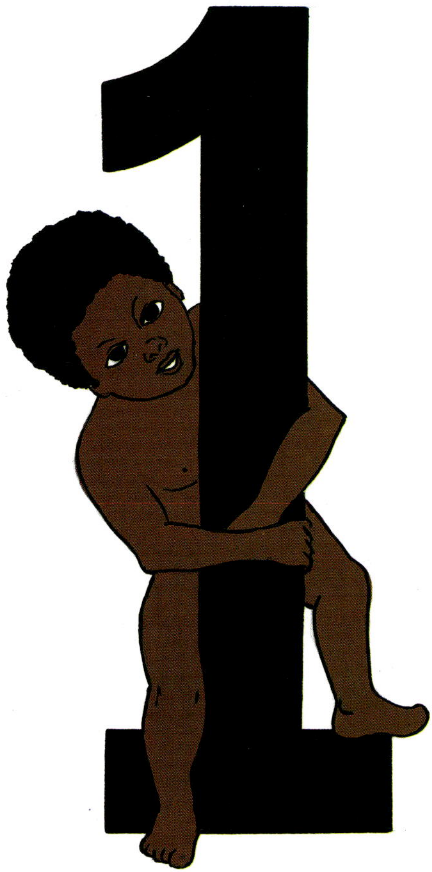

one

start the fun

count the balloon

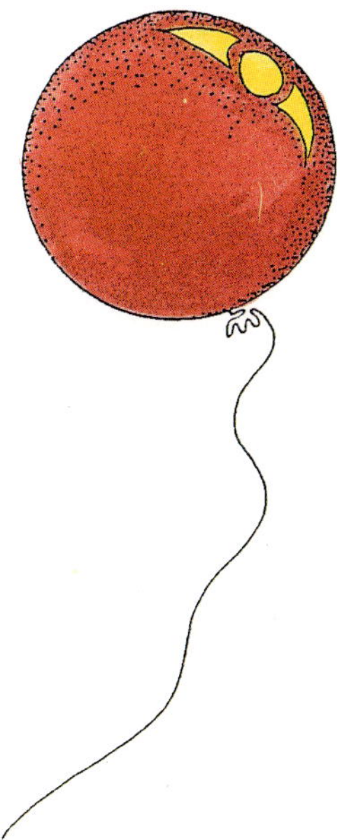

one balloon

two

buckle my shoe

count the shoes

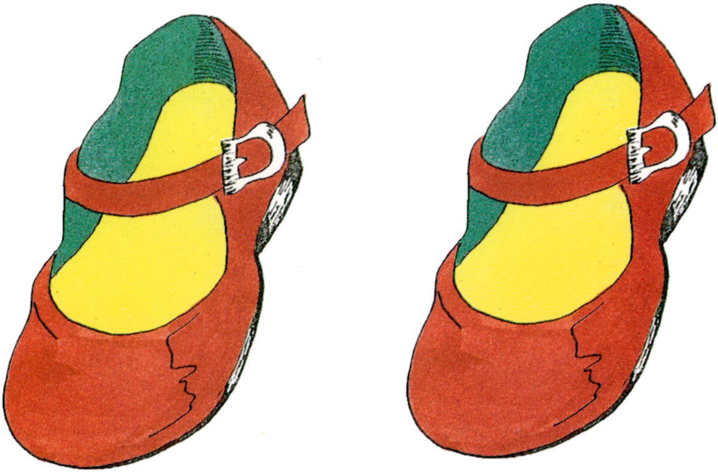

two shoes

three

climb a tree

count the trees

three trees

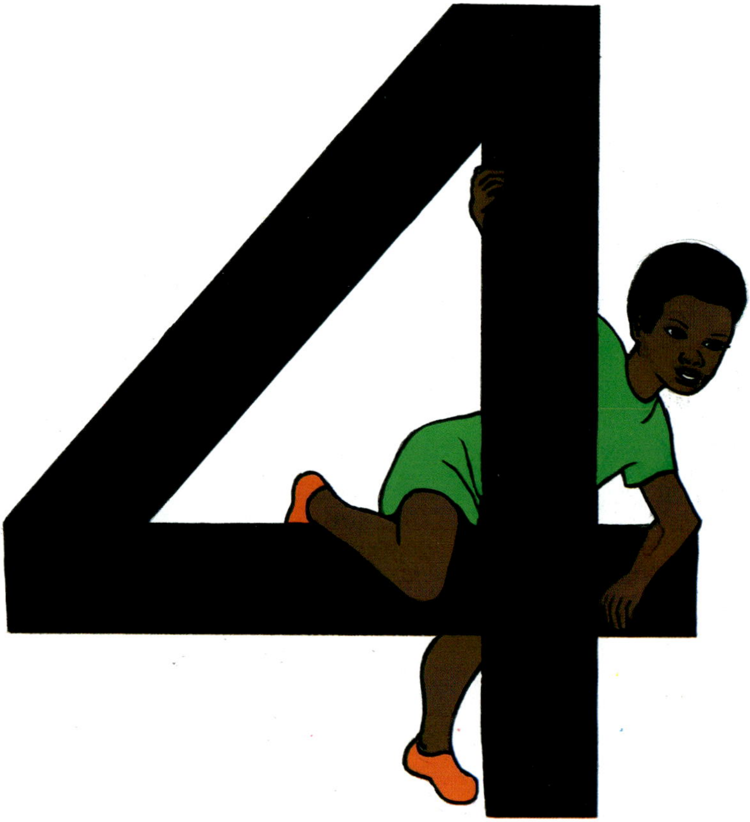

four

open the door

count the doors

four doors

five

jump and jive

count the maraccas

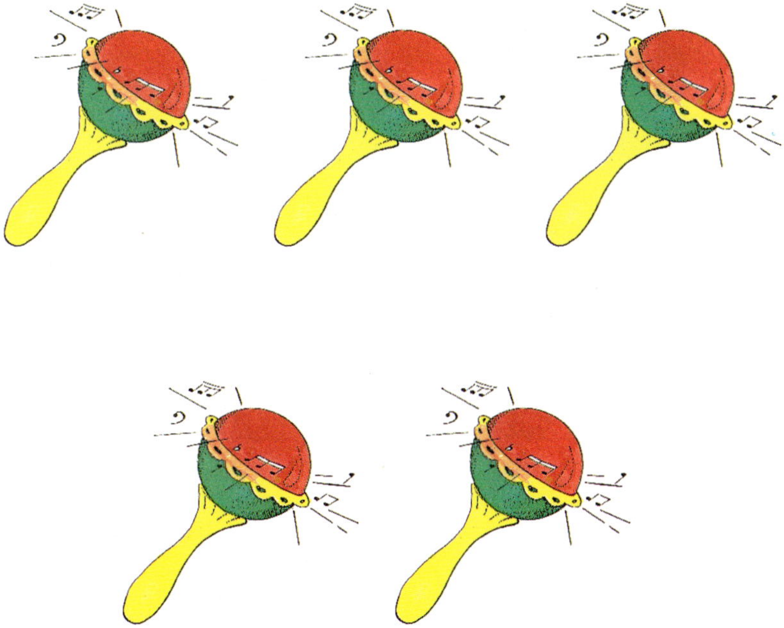

five maraccas

six

pick up sticks

count the sticks

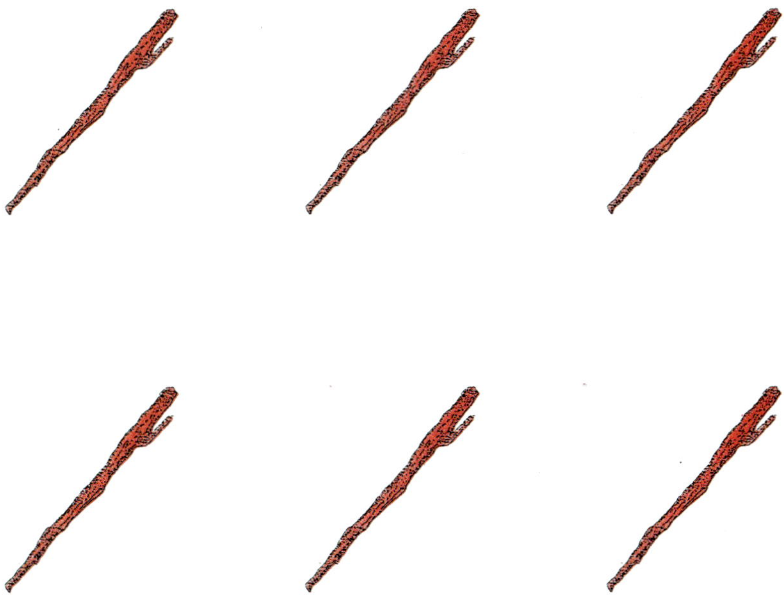

six sticks

seven

swing up to heaven

count the swings

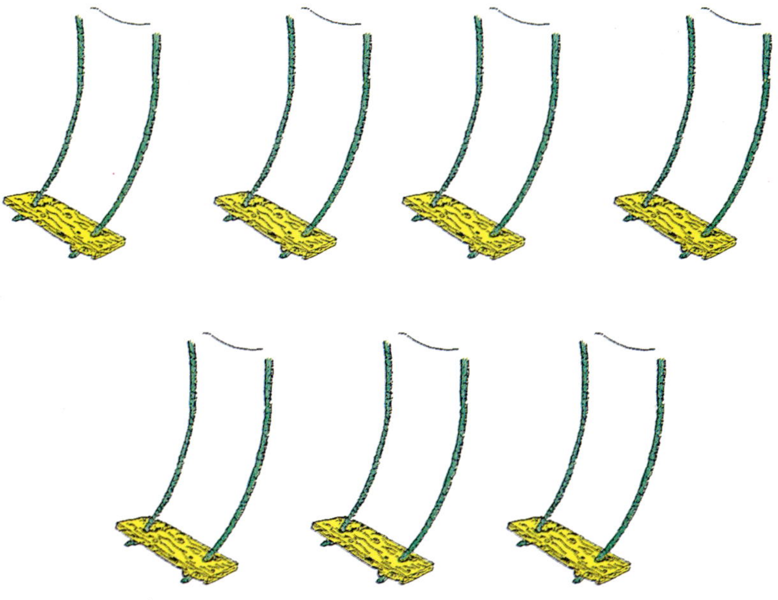

seven swings

eight

stay up late

count the skates

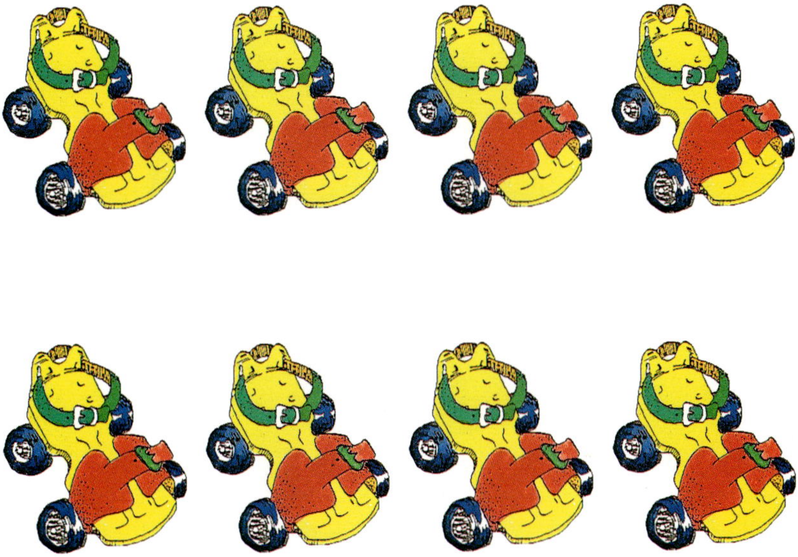

eight skates

nine

what is the time

count the clocks

nine clocks

ten